It Will Always Be A Cage

Mari Monroe

This book might not be for everybody.

But it might be for somebody.

That is enough.

Table of Contents

For my family, blood and beyond.

Oof, first book.

I love you.

Preface

As you navigate this book, I hope it will serve as a portal into your own soul, your own mind, and your own heart. I hope you find little pieces of yourself tucked between these pages. I hope that the same words which bleed from my heart, melt into yours- kindred spirits. I hope that the lines that litter these poems offer a mirror, a reflection, for you to look into and understand that it's all okay, everything you feel, everything you have felt, it's all okay.

In words, we can find self-expression and in self-expression we can find purpose and in our purpose we can find our soul, soft and at ease. So with that, I say speak, read, and write on.

Pour Me A Cup

Have you watched the way honey drips

from a jar?

It does not rush,

it keeps a steady course.

It is slow and magnetic,

And when it arrives-

everything is sweeter.

    -   Pour Me A Cup

We must learn to tolerate

The discomfort of healing

If we do,

in fact,

Wish to mend that which broke us.

- Band Aid

I spent my life mapping out the fastest

way to find treasure.

I wrapped my fingers in the finest

silver,

hoping to attract shiny objects that obey to

the sight of beauty,

But my heart always chased gold.

As I wandered,

the sterling began to serve

as a reminder

that whatever I decided to touch,

would always be second best

to that which rests beneath my skins

surface.

The gold I sought

Lived inside.

So I called off the search.

-    Finest Gold

I watch my shadow dance with your

steps-

we almost look like we are having fun.

But for me, in a very real sense-

you're not real,

a ghost-

that takes the shape of my whole body.

You are me,

and I love you,

but you are often not wanted.

You ruin some of the best moments.

-    Fake Smile

I promise to let go of that which doesn't
serve me,
But I can't promise it won't change me.
I think it is wise to learn from the
things we work to let go of,
I don't push it away with hopes of never
feeling it again.
I breathe it gone, intentionally.
A solution,
I am better off without that which
weighs me.

- A Promise

I ask my head,

What hurts?

But as always,

It redirects my question to the heart.

- No Stupid Questions

It is ok to celebrate

a step forward,

Even when

there are still miles to run.

- Marathon Not A Sprint

There are days when my fingers ache

trying to hold it all together,

Grasping for what cannot be contained.

But just as water puddles,

And then slips through my hands,

Happiness cannot be held.

It is tragically destined to only be felt.

- Fleetingly

I have felt fears that buckle my knees,

But similar to the way

wind pushes

through trees,

I will not waiver,

Crash or fall,

For my roots keep my grounded

And my spine keeps me tall.

- Nature's Giant

Note To Self

It's really about

allowing yourself to plant seeds

where you want to grow,

Not where others want to see flowers.

- Self Nourished

I love through you,

I love deeply, interwoven.

Messy and wild,

Blooming from untouched soil,

Then drowning.

- Category 4

And above all else,

I truly believe that there is

nothing

more risky

than pretending not to care.

Pretending not to love.

Pretending not to notice.

- So Why Do I Avoid A Stranger's Eye?

Dear little lotus,

Be enough for yourself,

So that when others judge you,

Or doubt your character,

Your radiance does not waiver.

Your shine does not dull.

In fact,

you'll beam brighter than before,

Once you polish off the mud

that was dulling you down.

- Bloom

Think of all the ways our brain tries

to protect our heart.

We use our mind as protection,

A shield,

When really our heart is our

most valuable weapon.

It doesn't need protection,

It needs to be let free,

It needs to love without barriers,

Without bondage.

It needs to bleed without a band-aid.

It needs to learn

to repair itself,

when harmed.

- Open Season

My courage lies

in having my heart

as an anchor

and my gut as the captain.

I have little fear for the waters ahead.

- Cut and Run

You know what can spread faster than

a wildfire

on a hot and windy day?

Feelings.

And much like a wildfire,

All it takes is one spark-

and then it's all over.

-    Drought

I must remember that I am,

on my own,

Enough.

That I, despite having another,

That I, in addition to life's circumstances,

Am whole.

- Note to Self

A love is only as strong as its potential

heartbreak,

And his soul

planted a grenade in my chest.

- Warned

The way roads are more dangerous

after a storm,

And people are warned

not to navigate

the rain-washed pavement,

That is how her heart works.

It feels unsafe after a heavy rain,

To the point where she doesn't feel

like driving much,

And if she waits long enough,

She will forget where her car keys hang.

- Subaru Sob Story

I Threw Out My Mirror Years Ago

You are a record with devastating
scratches.

I thought I buried you,
burned you.

Outplayed you.

You are old music, an old siren.

I've tossed you out multiple times!

How dare you come back.

But then you speak
and I listen.

I hang on to every word
you have ever spoken.

I let your words pierce through me.

You hug me while having arms spiked with
thorns.

I want to say stay away! But you know
I won't.

I listen.

I listen.

I know you are wrong,

- But You Often Feel Right

In a universe

where there are galaxies not discovered,

Waters not seen,

Planets not known,

In a world where there are seas to

swim,

Mountains to climb,

Sunsets to watch,

People to fall in love with...

You are choosing to focus on that one little

imperfection?

Borrow my glasses, dear.

-   Prescription Check

Allow yourself space and time

To prove to yourself that you are,

in fact,

Extraordinary.

You're other worldly,

Your soul is wildly

rogue.

Your heart exquisite.

Your mind a field of wildflowers.

Your thoughts a sea,

untamed.

You are the single only you that exists.

- Blossom

We're given a shell.

It's important,

I think,

to remind ourselves

that our shell is not everything that is

good about us.

- Body

Don't let love bleed

out from the cracks you've etched into

your skin from disapproval.

Instead, let love be the glue-

the tact,

that protects everything

from the outside

and binds

the once shattered

pieces back together.

- DIY

You are not limited.

Maybe you have put limits on yourself,

But you in your purest form,

are not limited.

I hope you see.

How the waves arrive,

without questions.

How the sun will set then rise,

Without restraint.

How years will pass without blinking.

So, to say that you are limited

or incapable,

Is to say that seasons never change,

Or the moon cannot outshine the sun.

So, I ask you- have you ever danced under

a full moon?

- We Wait For The Night

I am sorry if I cause hell,

it has never been my intention,

for my life

or anyone else's,

And yet here we are.

She whispers to herself.

-    In The Mirror

When a vessel gets bruised,

We do not blame the ocean-

We look instead on the weakness of the

ship.

Which is why when our heart is torn,

We feel unworthy of love,

We blame our own beating,

When really we could,

Instead,

Steer to calmer waters.

    -    Captain

Have you felt it?

True self love?

It's freedom.

Freedom from frowning in the mirror.

- I Threw Out My Mirror Years Ago

A reddish, orange-ish hue

Lives inside of you.

But first you must find a match,

To light it on your cue.

For a flame doesn't flicker without a

helping hand.

So look around your life

and find the ones who say,

Yes.

- You Can

Parched

We live and we learn.

But I feel honored to have learned

to live.

- No Cage

Tongue twisted nights,

Laced with wine,

Taste the same as a confessional.

Did I say too much?

Or not enough.

- Peace Be With Me

I'll allow a downpour any day,

If it means opening

opportunities that felt impossible

to crack.

Floods feed the desolate,

Giving life to what once ran dry.

-    Parched

Where's My Wrench?

I don't think it matters-

the kind of torture your heart is destined to
experience.

It all ends up feeling the same.

I have had it sneak up on me,

knock my feet out from under me.

It might have slammed me head-first,

had I not been keeping my eyes in the

hearts of others.

I have also had it where I saw it

coming,

I stared it down.

Neither circumstance you can prepare for.

It will come

and destroy you when it does.

But destruction is not the end.

You have been cracked, ripped, stabbed,
pulled, drowned.

But your heart?

- It Still Beats

It's a physical pain,

just as much as it is emotional,

The way your body crumbles,

even as you stand up straight.

You smile, teeth showing.

But the edges, dead,

cracked.

Nothing else can repair you-

but what you didn't see coming is that

you are a handyman in disguise.

You will repair yourself.

It may be slow, but one day you feel taller.

Well, until the next time.

But the next time it hits,

you will have a hammer and nail in your

back pocket.

-    Where's My Wrench?

Cracked or cursed,

Neither necessarily better or worse.

She screams,

that's the point.

We grow.

We accept what is

in order to move into

what will be.

A heart broken,

is a heart opened.

- Aortic Valve

It won't matter that progress isn't
linear,

It will only matter that progress exists,
it's attainable.

And with that mindset-
you can't lose.

- Full Heart

How do you leave someone who holds so

many pieces of your heart?

How do you detach your interlaced fingers

from someone else's

soul?

But with every tragic love,

Sometimes the winter comes early.

Snow will cover the footsteps of the

past,

And that love will feel a distant memory.

But spring will come,

and when it does.

- She Smiles

Between Us

Hello, my personal darkness.

You sneak your way through partly cracked doors,

The kind that we often gently close,

not thinking to check the latch behind.

But you find your way in,

silently, unannounced.

You know you are never welcome,

and that is what makes your unwanted

return so sweet

to you.

You feed off of guilt and shame.

You're thirsty for self-loathing and torment.

You greet hurting souls with open arms!

You hold hearts, knowing damn well they are ticking time bombs in your hands,

When really they are meant to be soft wings in our chests that allow the beating of blood to be our reason for waking up each morning.

You seep into our bloodstream as easily as water takes up salt,

you dissolve and inhabit our entirety.

You twist your fingers into our thoughts, controlling with painful force- the opposite of how our minds wished to be held- which makes your presence that much more uncomfortable.

You don't fit.

But similar to the way a puzzle is not complete even with one missing piece of 1,000,

You slide yourself in, forcing your sharp edge into a rounded corner,

You create a fake wholeness.

We know ways to break your bond,

We know tools that pry you from our beings,

But for some, you are intoxicating to the point where we do not know who we are,

without you.

Hello, my personal darkness.

You are not always around,

In fact, I am quicker now, at banishing you away.

But on the days where you come back- I am surprised to still know you by name.

Hello, my personal darkness.

I have been coerced into greeting you like
an old friend, time and time again.

So, maybe,

not now,

but someday- I will be able to wave at you
from afar.

Acknowledging you are still there,

but allowing distance to separate your dark
shadow from my own.

The distance that should be,

must be built.

- Between Us

Simple things are glass,

beautiful and delicate,

But oh!

If you could hear the symphony my

heart orchestrates?

Shattered pieces.

You'd dance like a fool.

A Mad Hatter in his own world,

not stuck in Wonderland.

Just be mindful of your step,

watch out for the shards-

glass once shattered-

Now whole,

With a live edge.

Seemingly smooth to touch,

But one false stroke and I will watch

You.

- Bleed

An easy mistake it is,

To convince yourself of falsehoods that

live deep within you.

I urge you to lift the veil

you have punished yourself with.

I will show you how blurred your vision

has been.

That you are beyond.

Beyond loved,

Beyond worth every ounce in which this

life has to offer.

- Worthy

Have you ever felt rain on your skin,

Only to look up to see bright

blue skies?

You realize,

It's in your eyes.

- Storm Warning

This woman has cried tears that put

the ocean to shame.

This woman has felt pain,

unbearable to human touch.

This woman has climbed mountains

only to reach a summit with no view.

This woman has been left confused,

alone, betrayed-

Yet she walks,

No runs,

Towards love, towards life.

This woman is me- but she is also you.

She is your brother, your sister, your
mother.

She is your uncle, your cousin, your
neighbor.

She is humanity at her finest, and human
at her realest.

    -   Real Strength

My Will

We will hurt,

but we will heal. We will hurt,

but we will heal. We will hurt,

but we will heal. We will hurt,

but we will heal. We will hurt,

but we will heal.

- My Will

I know you hear the words before

they come out of their mouth.

She is speaking a language that I can

no longer understand,

But translate seamlessly into knives.

I feel them,

blades in my chest.

- Grief

A day after.

A week after.

A month after.

3 years after.

The heaviness stays,

even when I feel light.

Even when I smile, I dance.

The heaviness stays,

We were meant to be enemies.

But you have long since become a comfort.

I breathe.

How is it that pain becomes a

familiar friend?

- Uncommon Friendship

There is power in knowing

when to pick up the rope,

And wisdom in knowing when to let go.

Just as there is strength in holding on,

But release when you accept

that not all things are meant to be held.

- I Look At The Scars On My Hands

It's drowning, drowning, drowning.

It's more drowning.

It's drowning, drowning, drowning.

You're uncertain of how you are breathing.

All you feel is the drowning.

All you know is the drowning.

All you are comforted by is the drowning.

All you hate is the drowning.

It's more drowning.

Until it's less.

And one day it will be less.

-   I Was Only Walking

A Forest of Anything

I knew I was in love with the wind

when I saw it ruffle the golden grass

that covered my backyard.

It sang a song that sounded a lot like peace,

and tasted like warm milk

with cinnamon.

My 7 year old self knew then what love

felt like.

Love was adventure and raw beauty

wrapped into every landscape that I

hoped to run across.

It was in every leaf that grew

and fell.

It was in every cloud

that covered my head.

- Naive

Be a seed to build a forest.

Plant.

Hydrate.

- A Forest Of Anything

The Moon raised her voice softly,

And asked the Sun

if she could join her for the early hours

of the morning.

Just to see the early birds gaze up from

their coffee cups,

And greet them both.

- Old Friends

It's Nature's way of saying, "You can do this!"

When the sun rays hit an oceans skin,

When the first orange leaf pops from a green forest,

When rain hits your eyelids unexpectedly.

It's in the little moments,

that life wants us to wake up.

- Divinity

Uninvited

Why is it weak to say that I am in pain?

Didn't that take courage?

Allowing past hurt to fall from tear ducts,

It is

quite the journey,

one I did not ask for.

- Uninvited

It's a strange thing to navigate

emotions that not a single word in the

English language,

Or multitude of,

Can begin to construe and define.

Though I guess you have taught me to

trust feelings more than words,

For your words became lies,

now lost,

And my emotion has become

my

anchor.

- Trust

When the fear that is weighing us

down,

Can be lifted,

Even if only by an inch,

What a different world we would live in.

- Let My Shoulders Rest

She took deeper breaths,

Not really understanding how,

Honestly not noticing

at all that *they*

were whole.

But others noticed,

And she began to feel it.

Her chest, heart, head,

Felt lighter.

Her body and spirit and soul were able

to breath again,

And little else mattered in that moment.

Shackles were cut.

Ones she didn't know she was wearing.

- Pranayama

To be so sad that it hurts to lift your
eyelids.

To be so hurt that your heart
exhausts itself with every beat.

To be so lost that no compass could
guide you.

To feel consumed by darkness to the
point of forgetting.

That is where healing might start.

-    Heal

Allow yourself grace in growing pains.

No one judges nature's mud when a

storm hits,

For we know with the rain,

Flowers will bloom.

- Which Seed Did You Plant?

I Wear Two Weapons

Look at the way silence can fill cups of
coffee,
Or perhaps it's how stillness sits in
your tea.
It's quite possibly the most beautiful
form of listening.

- What's In Your Cup?

I've wrapped my soul

In something I deem magic.

It was hard to lasso down,

She was a mystery.

I was unsure.

But I've tucked her into every crevice of

my body.

Every hidden nook.

Every drop of blood.

She blankets me when I need comfort

and supports me when I need freedom.

I've named this magic Gratitude.

I didn't know her at first,

But she's kept me company now for a

long time-

And she has sat with me through some of

my darkest pages.

So I ask you,

What magic drapes your soul?

- Blanket

Water your roots today,

So that blossoms are here by Spring.

- Roots To Branches

Trace the lines of your mind,

Intimately and delicately.

Focus on what lies within first,

Sit with the girl crying in your chest.

And then turn your attention onward.

And discover where she leads you.

- Map

Mindfulness isn't about silence or
stillness.

It just means that in all the chaos,

In all the movement of your mind or

within your body,

And within your breath,

You're choosing the present moment,

Over and over again.

What a sweet space to live.

- Now

I am stronger than the energy around me,

For I have the energy within.

- Me

I have etched the meaning of happiness
into my skin so deeply,
So that when I cut wounds out
of the corners of pain and forgiveness,
And replace them with the respect of
healing,
I am met with blood that flows.

-    Like Freedom

I wear two weapons at all times,

One stays hidden,

One seeks all crime.

The one that hides usually finds our way,

I call her my brain,

For she will never betray.

The one that seeks,

demands to be seen.

She clings from my sleeve,

The head of the team.

The three of us together never stray apart,

For we are led by our leader,

I call her my heart.

- I Wear Two Weapons

Wild

I hadn't brushed my hair in a couple of
days.
I hadn't thought about my hair in that
same amount of time,
when my best friend mentioned it
as she combed the hair of her American
Girl doll.

How could I care about the silk of my
hair,
When there were hills to roll down?
How could I care about combing
dolls hair,
When my brother often wore a frown?
At 6 years old I experienced what it felt
like to be the wild one.
The next day I chopped off my Barbie's hair.

- I Cared Enough

To be strong and gentle.

Fierce and kind.

Loyal and bold.

To have a voice and open ear.

To speak up and listen intently.

To sit and observe or get up and walk out,

both viable.

To nurture and empower.

To be all in one

and everything in

between is to be.

- A Woman

I am dancing

without knowing the steps.

Two left feet,

But a grin ear to ear.

I hope you dance, too.

Boldly, with feeling.

So I remind you,

and I will remind you as often as I can,

What a shame it would be,

To sit it out.

- Two Left Feet

She was a mess of color,

full of wildflowers

taped to pages remembered,

Pine scented forests

and the mud beneath her feet.

She was a little bit of let it be,

And a little bit

be the change

you wish to see.

    -    Lily

I promise to always be kind,

Patient,

Wild.

I promise to look up at the stars more,

And at my feet less.

I promise to love genuinely,

Fearlessly,

I promise these things for myself,

first.

And I wish these things for others.

-    Always

She is here, blindly and ragged.

Be here, too.

Be here, wildly.

Be here, unapologetically.

Be humble, fiercely.

Because her two favorite questions were

"why?" and "why not?"

- Never How

Let your feet lead you fearlessly and

effortlessly down dirt roads,

Let your core be shaken and loved,

All in the same breath.

Let your lungs fill not only with

mountain air,

But with the scent of all the bravery

and courage that exists around you and
within you.

Let your exhales be long,

Thoughtful,

And messy- allowing escape for that

which doesn't belong to you.

Let yourself be the calm,

And the storm,

And everything.

-    In Between

Be the sweet honey,

Be the salt sea.

Or simply,

Darling girl,

Be whatever you wish to be.

- Whomever

Just like sweet daisies,

and sunflowers,

Just like a field of yellow that jumps

from mountain tops

high above.

She blooms where she pleases.

- Wild

She wished

to live as recklessly and

fiercely as the ocean.

No agenda, untamed.

And what she wished;

she became.

- A Hurricane

She was crowned with flowers,

That took the form of dreams and stars.

Her smile was scarred,

But it still lit up any room.

She was something fierce,

and she didn't have to prove it to

anyone.

She was a sight to see,

The color of blood, with a sweet scent.

She wore her thorns proudly.

- Rose

Like the sea,

She enjoyed wild chaos,

Undiscovered depths,

And sweet sun rays that kissed her

skin.

- Utopia

She is hot tea on a summers' day,

A sea breeze in mountain air,

She is not what she is supposed to be,

But what is fun about

predictability?

- You Are Not An Equation

It Will Always Be A Cage

At the end of each day,

Sometimes the beginning,

I allow myself to feel all that which

tears me apart.

I allow myself to feel everything that

sits heavily across my chest,

That of which feels like needles in my

stomach.

All of that which takes a blade to the back.

It is in allowing myself to feel all that

which rips me into pieces,

That I, in return,

Can count all of that which holds

me together.

- Japanese Bowl

Simply knowing the truth that

tomorrow is not promised,

Is enough to have boundless gratitude.

- Today

Today:

Another day to sip tea.

Another day to say hi to strangers.

Another day to smile at the small

things,

And laugh from the root of your belly.

Another day to be brave and say what's

on your mind,

And to listen to those around you.

Another day,

Another day,

Another day,

And that is all I could ever ask for.

- Can You Believe It!

It's a cage, it will always be a cage.

Unless you have eyes that see beauty in

the dirt roads that lead to nowhere.

It will always be a cage,

Unless you see dust particles dancing in
the light from your window and admire the
show.

It will always be a cage,

Unless you know that you are entitled to
that which brings you safety and love, but
you must also know that it will not feel safe
or lovely to everyone.

It will always be a cage,

Unless you fall madly in admiration for the
way waves crash along a shoreline,

The way snow blankets whole towns,

The way the sun kisses children's skin,
leaving freckles behind.

And it will always be a cage,

Unless you allow yourself grace in grief,

Unless you allow yourself time.

It will always be a cage,

Unless you allow yourself time- that cannot
and will not be rushed-

or taken for granted,

or wasted away.

It will always be a cage.

Unless you allow yourself time.

Unless you allow yourself time.

Unless,

You allow yourself, time.

Then

-   It Won't Always Be A Cage

The real challenge?

To not combat life's punches with resistance.

To not tense, deflect,

or suppress life's casualties.

You don't fix a sore muscle by adding tension.

If something hurts, more resistance isn't

going to help.

- Ice Or Heat

I flirt with allowing life to "happen",

while knowing full well that

I'm steering my own ship.

- Pass The Oar

May I ask this of you?

Work relentlessly to bring yourself

happiness.

Don't look for it in others.

Plain and simple-

you will not find it there.

You are your own

Happiness,

Beauty,

Love.

Not someone else's version.

- Original

I tucked my smile between the corners

Of "overwhelmed" and "unsure".

She hid there,

Thinking she was standing in solidarity.

Thinking that her presence wasn't

welcome to a revolution.

But as my legs marched forward,

She couldn't help but peek out from her

haven.

Now she stretches upwards,

Wider than before-

surrounded by

others who shared her presence.

It felt good to smile again.

This time for a cause that would last a

lifetime.

-    For Future Me

Don't you find that your heart

sometimes aches from being

surrounded by tongues

that talk too much,

but don't really say anything?

- Ear Sores

It's that time of year,

Where we are told that it is acceptable

to strip our layers,

Shed the weight of other's unwarranted

opinions,

And dive head-first into a new version

of whoever you want to be.

But I hope you learn,

that this molting of old skin can take

place at any time,

You need not wait for the turn of a

decade.

-    New Year

Sit with the split personalities of both
simplicity and chaos-
two conversations that life brings,
tied together with a simple ribbon of
mutual understanding-
they each will offer something magical that
the other does not possess.

- Match Made

It's a funny concept,

time.

It has no regard for humanity-

Yet we invented it.

Well played.

-    It's 4:54

Being content does not mean you have
no spark for an enthusiastic life.
It does not mean you have settled,
It does not mean you are complacent,
stuck,
unmoving.
It means you are okay with this present
moment,
And these days, I feel that a lot more
people should aim to be okay, first.
Be okay first, and happiness will catch up.

-   It Was Never A Chase

Free Rent

I have tucked parts of myself away,

Into foreign landscapes and cobblestone

streets,

where the language rings at a more

romantic frequency.

I've tucked parts of myself away into others'

arms and hearts, hoping to stay for a

lifetime.

I've tucked myself away in feelings that

Escape me as quickly as they came, but oh!

How lovely they felt.

What a beautiful problem it is,

to have too many homes.

- Free Rent

All We Have

I look at the sky and ask the stars

what's beyond them.

I'd like to think that they enjoy the view

of something grandiose.

Maybe they even enjoy the view of us,

little earth.

Or maybe it doesn't matter much at all

what the view is.

Let our eyes bleed beauty, that

is what they are made of.

Let our hearts experience kindness,

its single ingredient.

Let our souls be love, love, and love.

So I will keep watching the stars above,

in wonderment,

while simultaneously caring for my own

beauty.

- From Within

It's bloody, ok

to not know.

It's ok to have doubt,

It's ok to try

and not know what the

outcome is going to be.

It's ok to fail.

It's ok to fall.

I promise an answer will reveal itself at

the bottom,

or top,

of wherever you arrive.

- Move

You're an odd feeling; uncertainty.

I dance with you daily.

I am tormented by your indecisiveness.

Then when I try to pin you down and

make you speak and choose a side,

You go silent, numb, blind.

You shut all feeling off,

either to save me from the truth or to

torture me more without clarity.

I am not sure which one I'd prefer.

- Silent Sufferer

A little less old and a little less wise,

Will make a kid healthy, wealthy, and realize,

That if taken too seriously, a life might it waste.

Especially when believing in any other place.

To wish of something better is a foolish dream,

For any kid can see what adults haven't seen.

That life is in these moments,

the present, so true.

That time spent only today,

will allow a soul to renew.

- All We Have

What age is it that we start to forget our power?

Our wildness?

Our wonder?

Not that it's completely lost, but these qualities hide from us,

impersonating under different names;

Maturity,

Structure,

Adulthood.

I ask that you shed these layers of

unwanted titles and allow maturity to

feel like power.

For there to be wildness in your

structure,

And wonder in your adulthood.

- Peter Pan

Lined With Silver

I've traced each crack that splinters my
skin,

Wondering when I would be whole
again.

The lines divide what is old with what's
new,

Filled with impermanent pain and lost
love,

To name a few.

Each crack is a valley with depths
unexplored,

Each line is a story, some with little
reward.

But if you look closely, you will see new
skin blooms,

Over the old, all the hurt it consumes.

A new scar is formed, which will not let
us forget,

that our past is no fool, but our life is

- No Threat

She wrote to heal others,

To help in the smallest and most

impactful way she knew how.

She knew words could heal.

And she wished to give all the words

she could find,

away for free.

She did this from the fact that she

knew the world needed healing,

Starting with her own heart.

- Selfish Writer

She was ready to welcome the breeze

that would lift her soul.

She was ready for transformation.

She was ready for her wings,

Immaculate blue,

A Sight.

- It Is Your Turn To Fly

It's the small sips of coffee in the
morning,
The sun light through an open window,
allowing only a birds' song through.
It's in the car rides with the windows
down and your favorite song narrating
the moment.
It's in the seconds of when you run to a
stranger,
giving them the purse they left behind
at a restaurant.
It's in the hug between you and your
parent,
whom you haven't seen in a little bit too
long.
It's in these times that
I will open my eyes wider to the world
around,
And not allow my heart to shut it out.

-    20/20

I take two steps towards

fear,

My feet tremble and my heart races,

excitement and uncertainty swarm my

throat.

I take two steps toward fear's edge,

My eyes water and my mind says no,

Anxiety rushes into my chest.

I take two steps into fear,

My lungs expand and my eyes dilate,

Curiosity stings my gut.

I take two steps through fear,

My legs are grounded but my ribs

shelter my heart for a blow,

Uncertainty blinds my sight.

I take two steps past fear,

My eyes open and my heart rejoices,

I have found me again and I am even

more beautiful than before.

On this side of fear,

I cannot remember who I was before I

took my first two steps.

- Towards Fear

She has learned that when it all gets too
heavy,

Putting it down is no weakness.

It's a necessary skill that allows

Time

To build back the strength that it might

take,

And carry it,

This time,

With more care.

- Emotions Get Heavy

It's beautiful,

The way you wake up every morning.

That's it.

That is beauty.

Facing the world, when a part of you

doesn't want to.

- Brave

It might be time to shed your old skin,
Allow your surroundings to peel off
your armour,
You need no protection for what is to
come.
For as a snake does not fear its
environment for taking scales that no
longer serve,
It welcomes the change as naturally as
it breathes,
Be that wise creature.
Allow your page to turn without looking
back at the words that scraped you.

- Sticks & Stones?

I have learned that peace feels

A lot like being alone,

But never lonely.

   -    Lessons

I search each heart string delicately,

Combing through the rips and tears

With care.

Don't let it snag,

Or else an old scar risks reopening.

Stab, past heartache reborn.

I hesitate.

I want to apologize to each story that's been

torn, hurt,

Bruised.

But instead I whisper thank you.

You have made me love harder.

- Heart String

Like broken glass,

my heart is a masterpiece.

Clean up is necessary,

and repair takes

time.

- Don't Walk Barefoot

What a messy woven blanket,

The fabric of our lives.

- Sewn With Love

And when the storm was over,

Everyone danced,

New flowers bloomed,

And we all were gifted new beginnings.

- Lined With Silver

When I started down the path,

I didn't know its end.

But I found my power shifted back,

When in a mirror I saw a friend.

- Gemini

Did you notice that the world asked us to slow down?

We didn't listen.

So she screams.

- What Will It Take

I often wrap myself

away from the world,

Only in preparation to fly more vibrantly.

- Metamorphosis

I hold all that shattered my heart in my
hands,

Not to throw it all away,

But to see what edges cut me,

What feels heavy,

And what might, in fact,

Still be beautiful.

- All That Has Broken Me Has Also
  Built Me

This is usually where you might find an 'about the author' page or a list of all the other books I have written.

I entrust that by reading these pages, you probably know enough about what lives inside my heart.

As for future books, oh man am I working on it!

I appreciate you, tremendously.

Thanks for being here.

Made in the USA
Columbia, SC
06 February 2021